Wilton shows the uses of the
decorating
GW01606014
BASIQUE
Tel 0181 951 5088 / 5845
£8·99

drop flower tips...

instant blossoms with just one squeeze

A lavish wedding cake is trimmed with hundreds of rosy drop flowers. Pipe them ahead of time in royal icing.

1. Tint royal icing in varied shades of pink. Pipe about 350 tiny flowers with tip 23, about 200 with tip 224 and 15 with tip 2D. Add tip 2 centers.

2. Bake, fill and ice the 12" two-layer base tier, and top three single layer tiers using Round Mini-Tier pans. Position largest mini-tier layer atop 12" using dowel rods for support. With Cake Dividing Set, divide base and 8" tier into twelfths (mark sides midway).

3. Pipe bottom shell borders and top reverse shell borders with tip 224. Pipe tip 224 zigzag garlands from mark to

By tradition, the top tier is saved for the couple's first wedding anniversary. We don't figure it in with the number of servings.

mark on base tier, and "C"-scrolls on tier above with tip 129. Accent base tier garlands with tip 4 "C"-scrolls and mini-tier "C"-scrolls with tip 4 fleurs-de-lis. Attach flowers with a dot of icing. Trim with tip 352 leaves. Assemble two top tiers at reception. Serve three lowers tiers to 68 guests.

No decorating experience is needed to pipe realistic petalled flowers in scores of forms and sizes! These speedy flowers literally "drop" out of the decorating bag.

For dozens of flowers in just a few minutes, fit a 10″ or 12″ decorating bag with any of the tips shown on the next page. Fill it with royal icing. Attach wax paper to the back of a cookie sheet with dots of icing or tape.

Now hold the bag *straight up,* touch lightly to the surface of the cookie sheet and give a quick squeeze. Stop pressure and lift your bag away. Like magic, you have a star-like flower. For swirled flowers (shown): Just curve wrist around to the left and, as you squeeze out icing, bring hand back to the right.

Turn the page for more about drop flower tips.

drop flower tips

Drop flower tips are members of the star tip family. Any star tip, open or closed, will pipe a pretty flower. Many of the star cut tips pipe well-formed flowers, too.

True drop flower tips have a center rod within the cone-shaped tip. This pipes a ring of petals with an open center. Fill the center with a dot, or pull out a cluster of stamens with a small round tip.

Here is just a sampling of the dozens of tips that pipe drop flowers. All are shown in actual size. Practice piping flowers with them, then use other star tips for flowers with a different look. There are lots of ideas in *Volume Three, The Wilton Way of Cake Decorating.*

All tips are shown in actual size

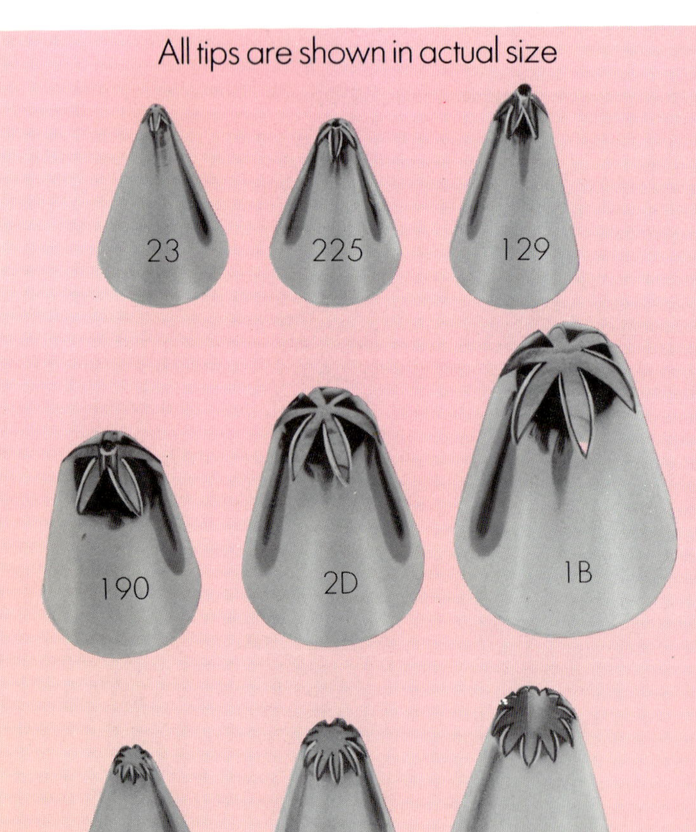

Tips for small flowers. Frame clusters in piped ovals or heart shapes, add stems and tiny leaves. Cover a puffy piped garland with these little blooms.

Tips for large flowers. Use these tips for flowers as large and impressive as many of those piped on a flower nail. Arrange them on cakes in sprays and groups.

Stellar tips pipe daisy-like flowers. Add tips 502 and 508—pipe perfectly matched blooms in five sizes. Perfect for tier cakes.

At right, in actual size, we show a sampling of flowers piped with drop flower tips. See the variety in size and form! Vary your colors, add center stamens with a small round tip. You'll be proud of your drop flowers!

ainty drop flowers in actual size

23

225

129

amatic drop flowers in actual size

aduated stellar drop flowers with
isy-like forms

drop flower tips pipe clear-cut shells, sculptured curves, deeply ruffled garlands.

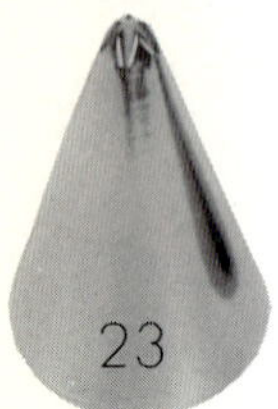

Use tip 23 for daintiest of trims

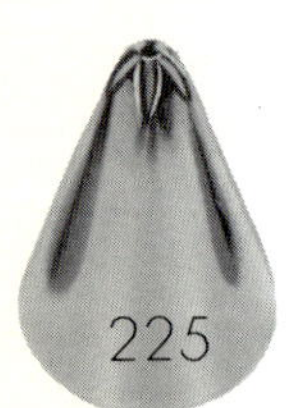

Precise forms with tip 225

Tip 129 for mid-size borders

Tip 190 for quick-to-add trims

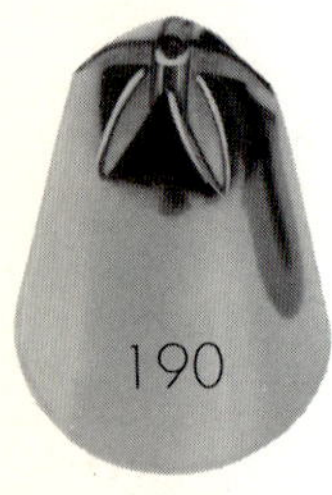

All trims and tips shown actual size.

Tip 2D pipes bold, dramatic forms

Tip 1B does a giant "C"-scroll

Stellar tips, identically cut, give unity to a tier cake.

drop flower tips

pipe fancy borders for distinctive cakes

Before piping decorations, measure and mark your cakes carefully—then you'll have an easy guideline to follow.

And don't overlook cookie cutters as patterns— they're quick ways to assured success.

Lightly imprint a heart cutter and use a stellar tip to form design. Add tip 132 drop flowers and tip 352 leaves.

Tip 504 pipes a ruffly garland. Cover garland with tip 225 drop flowers.

Pipe bold tip 131 rosettes. Add tip 129 drop flowers.

Use these suggestions to add bold, beautiful trims to your cakes in a jiffy.

leaf tips are indispensable, naturally

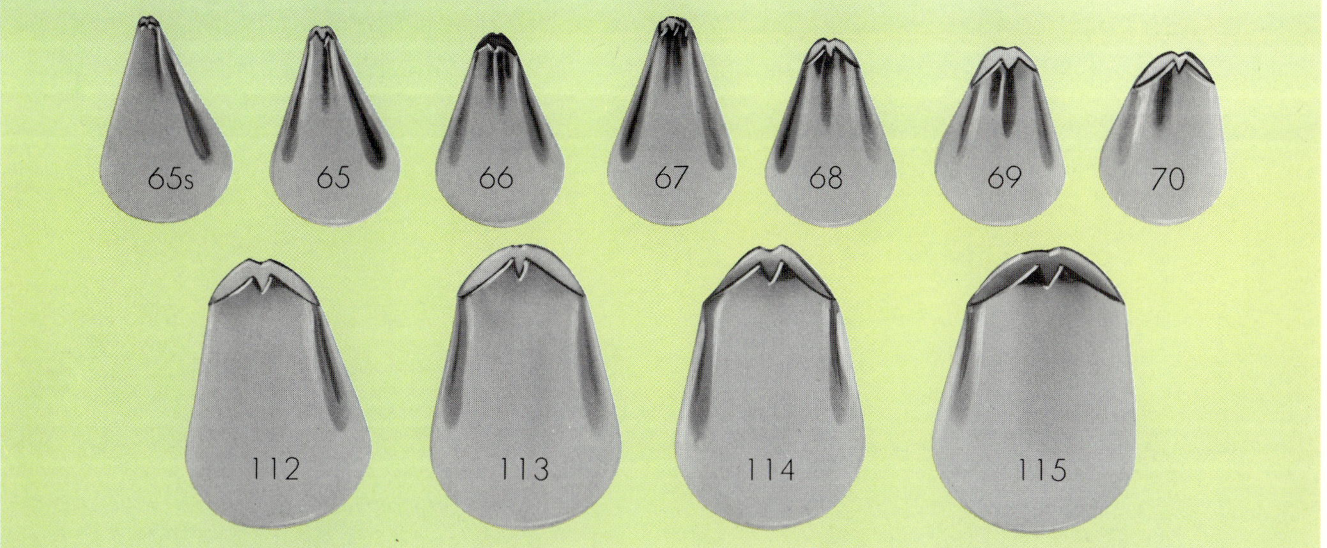

There's a wonderful range of sizes in leaf tips, from tiny tip 65s to giant tip 115.

To pipe a leaf, first attach flower to cake with a dot of icing. Now fit a parchment cone or decorating bag half-filled with icing with a leaf tip. Tips 67 and 69 are frequently used. Insert tip below flower petal and pull out leaf. This makes a smooth leaf. For a ruffled one, move your hand up and down. For a nice point, thin your icing with piping gel or light corn syrup. You will need to experiment for the ideal amount—start with one teaspoon per cup of icing.

Leaves piped with standard and giant leaf tips. All are actual size.

leaf tips pipe decorative borders

Leaf tips can be used to pipe more than just leaves. The simplest of motions will achieve lovely and unusual border designs—tiny and bold—when you use these versatile tips. The same motion will pipe forms that are identical except for size.

Large curve border. Use tip 114 and move your hand up and down gently to pipe a bold border for the side of a cake. For a dainty curve border, use tip 66. To elaborate on this border, repeat it two or more times, one set of curves above another.

Double ruffle scallop border. As with all borders, measure and mark your cake, midway on side. Connect marks with drop string guidelines, then use tip 70 to pipe a ruffled scallop, moving your hand back and forth for the ruffled effect. Choose a contrasting color and tip 66 to pipe a second ruffle on top of the first.

Straight beaded ruffle. Pipe a ruffle around cake side or top edge with tip 70. Go back and add a row of beads in the center with the round tip 3.

Bold leaf design. Use giant leaf tip 113 to pipe a row of rounded leaf shapes around the side of the cake. As you begin each shape, lift the tip to achieve a rounded, dimensional effect. Trim the border with tip 66 leaves, then add tip 225 drop flowers.

Leaf trio border. Run a tip 504 line around the side of your cake. Pipe trios of tip 66 leaves on it, then trim with tip 23 drop flowers.

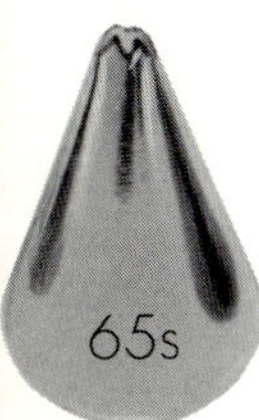

Tailored scallop is similar to leaf trio. Pipe simple tip 65 scallops all around the cake side, then add triplets of tip 70 leaves. Accent with tip 224 drop flowers.

Tailored zigzag makes a nice border for a man's cake. Just pipe a tip 70 zigzag all around the side of the cake, then add made-ahead tip 23 drop flowers.

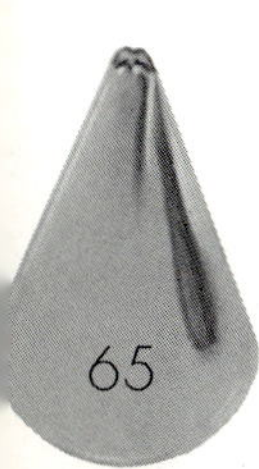

New curving vine. Pipe tip 65s "C" curves all around side of cake. Add tip 66 leaves.

Happy
Birthday
Ann

leaf tips are marvelously creative!

Decorate a spectacular cake for a birthday! This is a 10″ round two-layer cake. Fill and ice smoothly. Then divide in twelfths and mark at top and bottom edges, as shown. Write message with tip 3. Pipe tip 504 line around base and top borders, tip 113 leaf trios and attach royal icing drop flowers. Add candles in holders and serve to 24 guests.

They pipe flowers, too!

Some flowers can only be done with a leaf tip. You will need to do these flowers on a flower nail—a two-piece one is best. Use the size nail that corresponds to the size flower you wish to pipe. Line with foil and lightly cover with vegetable oil spray.

Bluebell. Use a bag half-full of royal icing. Placing your tip as deep as possible within the lined nail—pull out five evenly spaced petals, drawing each to a point using tip 67. Pipe a tip 13 star in center of flower—insert artificial stamens. Lift out foil for flower to dry, then line nail again.

Lily. Use royal icing—bag half full. Place a 68 tip deep within throat of nail and pull out six evenly spaced petals, bringing out to points. Pipe a tip 14 star in center of flower and insert artificial stamens.

petal tips make flowers and pretty trims.

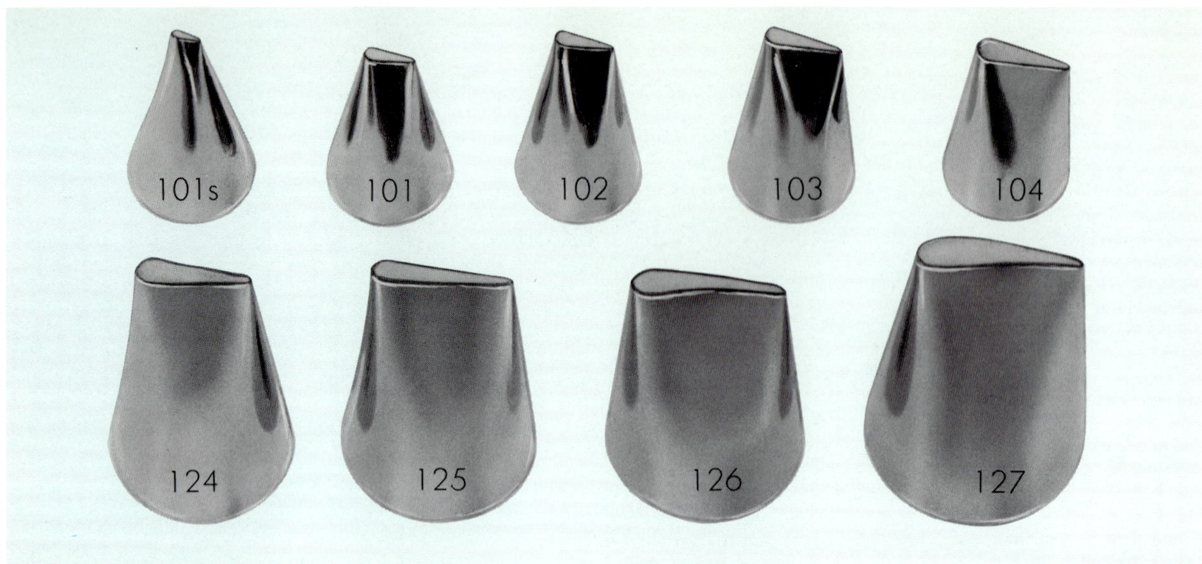

The petal tips are the most fun for decorators—they can reproduce almost any flower and do lots of ruffly trims.

The standard petal tips are identical, except for size. Each has a teardrop-shaped opening. The broader, rounded end is held against the surface to provide a strong base for the petal or ruffle. The narrow, pointed side is held outward and gives a delicate edge to the petal.

As you can see on the next page, just vary your petal tip to pipe flowers of various sizes. We suggest piping almost all flowers in royal icing, on waxed paper. When dry, attach with dots of icing. Royal icing flower details are sharper, colors are clear, and flowers may be stored almost indefinitely. For cake-top flowers, you may pipe in buttercream, then freeze or air-dry and place directly on the cake top just before serving.

A charming border is put together with a tip 125 ruffle, 101 roses and 101s forget-me-nots.

flowers are petal tips' most important use.

These tips pipe blooms of almost any size or variety quickly, accurately, easily. Of course, your own pressure control also determines the size of the flowers.

Tip 125 pipes big dramatic flowers, ideal for large tiers or good-sized cakes.

Tip 104 is the standard-size petal tip. Arrange the piped flowers in groups and clusters.

Tip 101 pipes dainty blooms for delicate cakes. Arrange them on cupcakes, petits fours, place them in round or oval frames to form borders.

petal tips pipe curving forms

Simple swag. Measure and mark your cake midway on side, then pipe tip 102 tailored swags. Good idea for a man's cake.

Ruffle. Simply measure and mark your cake on side, then pipe ruffly scallops with tip 124. Simple but festive. Add flowers, if desired.

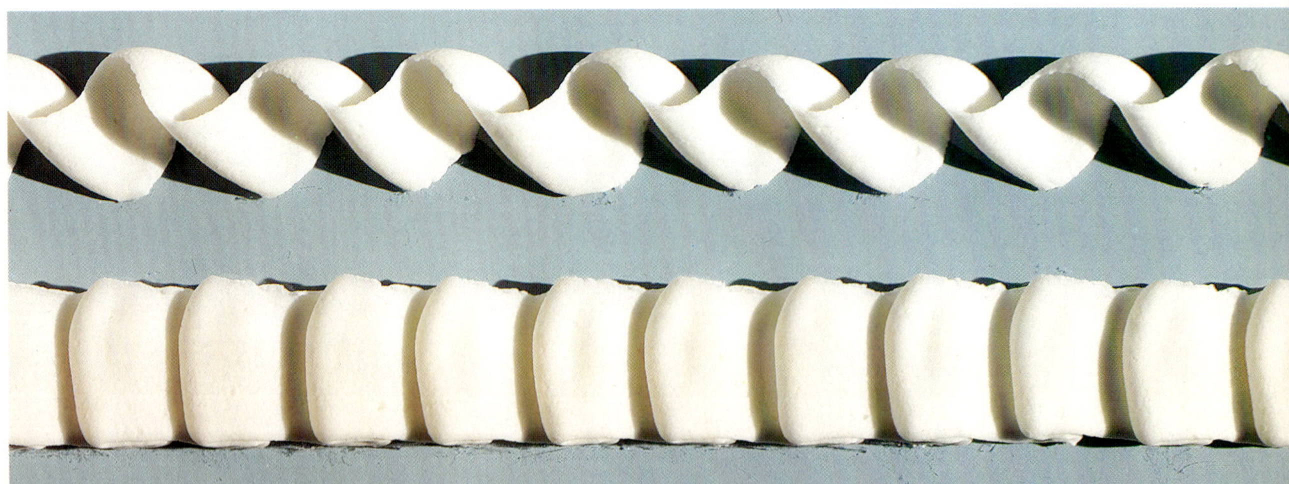

"U" border. Use tip 124 and an up-and-down movement of your hand to pipe this tailored border.

Pleated border. Pipe a series of overlapping shells with tip 126 for a tailored effect on top or bottom edge of cake.

borders quickly piped with petal tips

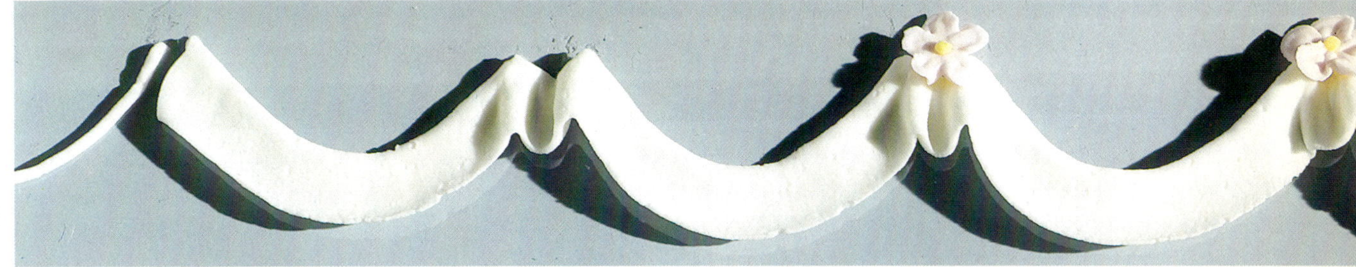

Rhythm swag border. Traditional and graceful. After marking your cake side midway, pipe tip 102 simple swags all around, dividing them with a short up-and-down movement of your hand that adds a triple indentation. Trim with flowers.

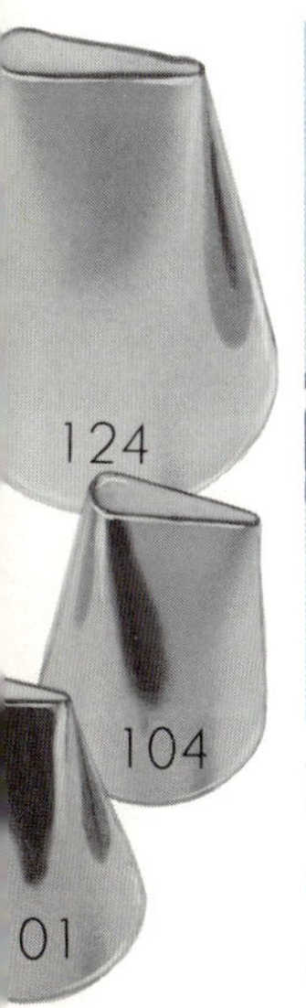

Double ruffle. Measure and mark your cake midway on side. Pipe tip 124 scalloped ruffle all around, add tip 104 ruffles and accent with tip 101 fleurs-de-lis. Color contrast adds to the effect.

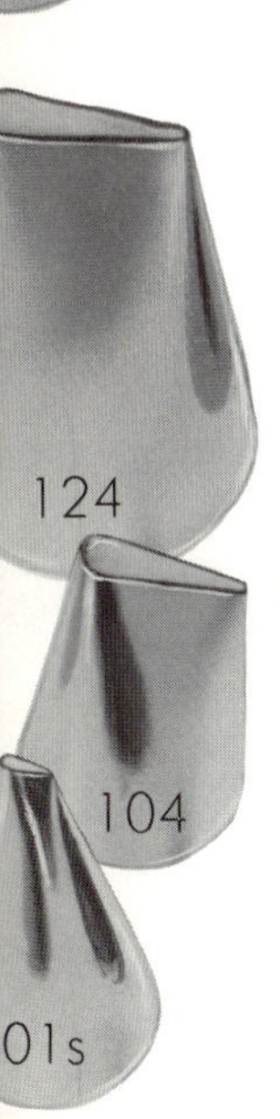

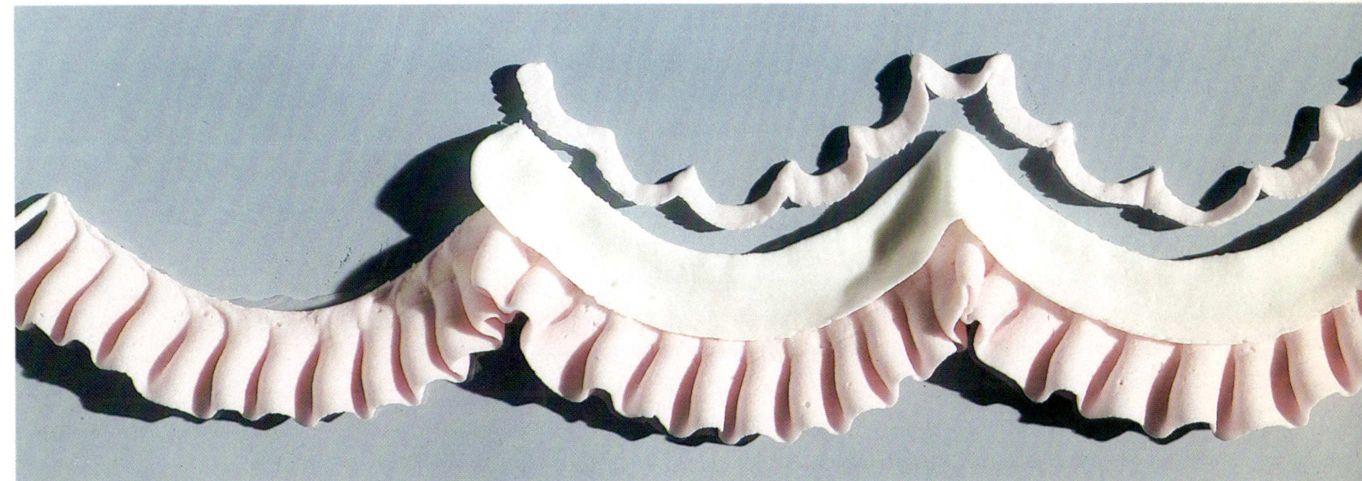

Ruffled swag starts with a tip 124 ruffled scallop, top it with a tip 104 swag and finish with dainty tip 101s scallops.

Good Luck
Jennifer

petal tips create a blossoming cake

What could be prettier than a petal-shaped cake adorned with a dainty spray of flowers! Make it for a birthday, retirement, or just a party. Bake a two-layer cake in 12" petal pans, fill, and ice smoothly. Using royal icing, pipe tip 125 roses, 103 daisies, 101 violets. Pipe tip 2 message. It's not necessary to measure and mark the cake—the petal shape does that for you.

Pipe a tip 124 triple ruffle around base of cake, single ruffle at top edge. Add tip 104 bows. Let cake icing dry. Arrange flowers in a spray on cake top, add tip 70 leaves. Serve cake to 28 guests.

Flower nails produce beautiful flowers
These helpers are essential for truly professional cakes. Fill a parchment cone or decorating bag fitted with the petal tip of your choice half full of royal icing. (Choose the tip that comes closest in size to the flower you want to pipe.) Now hold nail by its stem, using it like a tiny turntable turning counter-clockwise as you pipe a realistic flower. We recommend you use royal icing. Then you can work ahead, dry your flowers and have them ready to arrange on decorating day.

round tips pipe exquisite forms

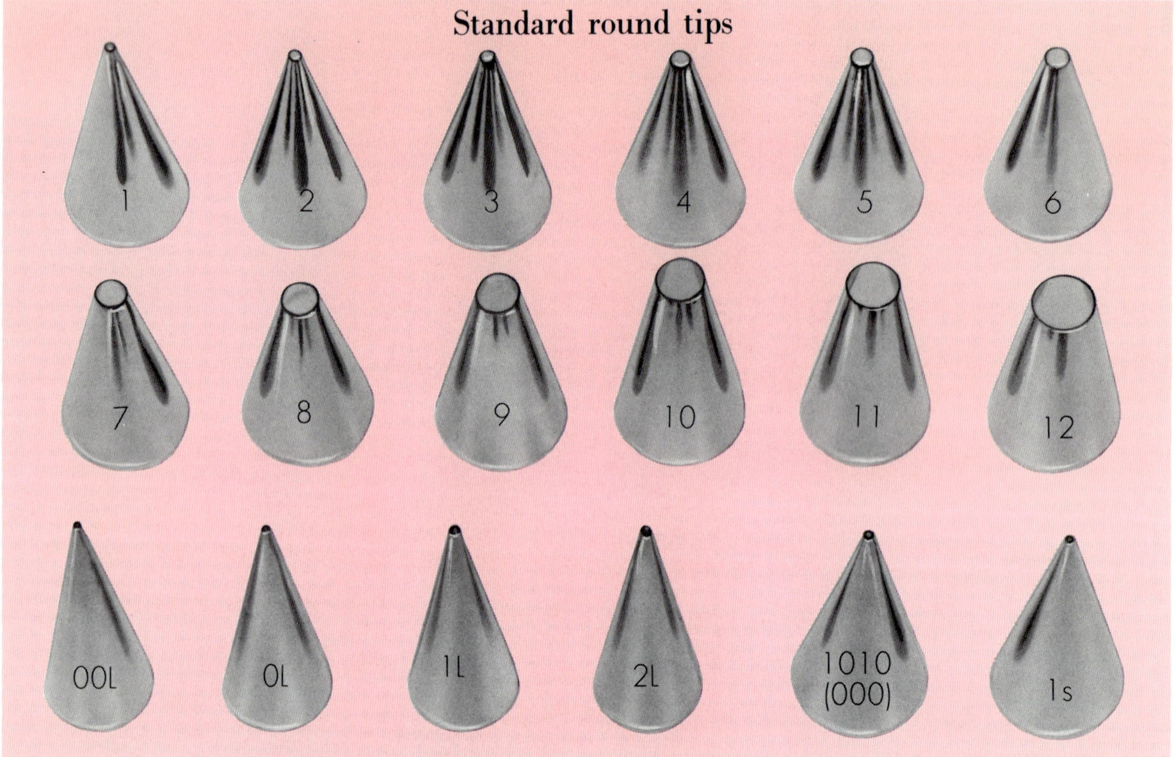

These round tips range from a very tiny 1s to a large 12, but all have the same round opening characteristic of these tips.

Lattice Crowned Shower Cake
Lattice can be quite versatile. On this beautiful cake, impressive lattice hearts are dried on flower formers to create an elegant crown for the top tier.

Trace four 3″ hearts on waxed paper. (Hint: Use a cookie cutter.) Tape patterns on 2″ wide flower formers (convex side). Cover hearts with tip 2 royal icing lattice and tip 1 bead borders. Let dry. Make 40 tip 23 drop-flowers with tip 2 centers.

Bake, fill and ice two-layer tiers—6″ x 3″, 12″ x 4″ round and 9″ x 3″ hexagon on cake circles, boards, Tuk-N-Ruffle and 10″ separator plate. Dowel rod and stack tiers. Divide and dot mark top tier into 6ths, base tier into 12ths corresponding with hexagon.

Pipe tip 2 double drop strings on 6″ sides. Edge tops with tips 4, 6 and 8* reverse shell borders; edge bases with tips 5, 8 and 9* bead borders. Edge plate with tip 6 beads. To make lattice garlands on hexagon and 12″ cakes, connect dot marks with tip 2 drop strings. Use tip 5 (on hexagon) or 8 to pipe bead garlands, three layers deep. Add tip 1 lattice. Edge lattice with tip 1 beads. Add tip 1 bows, dots and bead flowers. Attach hearts and flowers with icing. Assemble tiers with 5″ Corinthian Pillars, Petite Bells & Buds, Filigree Heart and Musical Trio figures. Serves 40. *Use smaller tips on top layer.

round tips pipe elegant designs

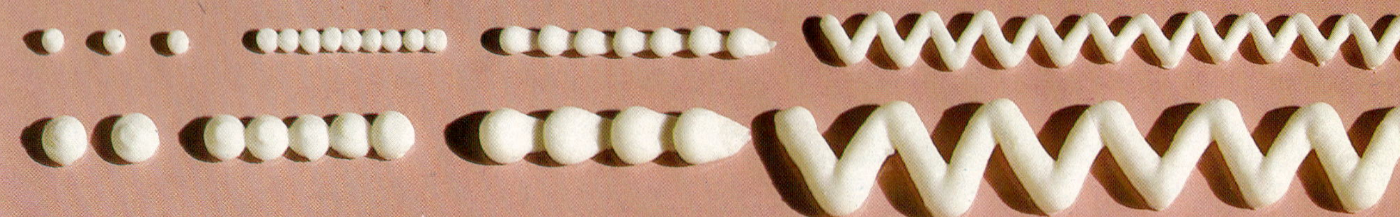

Dots. Pipe a row of tip 3 dots. Pipe them close together for a neat beaded edging. Use a larger tip for a ball border. Pipe shells instead of balls for a bulb border, and a wide zigzag for a "v" border—the possibilities are almost endless.

Delicate lattice is so impressive. One of the most dramatic ways to use it is to bridge it from the cake to a bold bulb garland. Be sure to measure and mark carefully before piping latticed garlands.

Round tip lettering. To achieve spectacular results when lettering on a cake, remember to measure and mark your cake so the message fits. Thin the icing with piping gel or corn syrup so it flows easily out of the bag. Use tips 1, 2 or 3—the smaller the tip, the more delicate the effect.

Happy BIRTHDAY

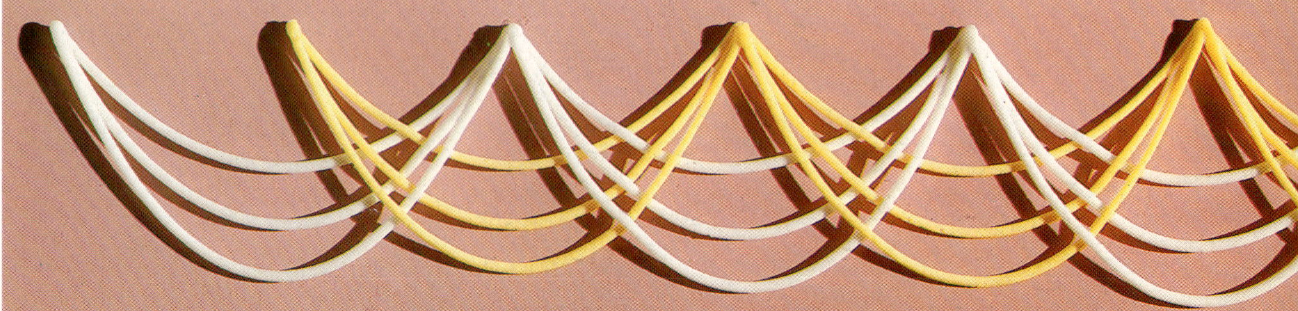

Interlace swags. Measure and mark your cake side, then drop tip 2 strings in alternating colors—first yellow then white, for an interlaced effect.

round tips have a sense of humor

Figure piped icing decorations are easy to do and delightful to see. Icing consistency and pressure control are essential. With a little practice, you'll soon be squeezing out adorable creatures, zany clowns and more. To create our magical menagerie, just use large or medium round tips to pipe the bodies, medium size for heads, legs, wings and ears; small for facial features and details.

Chicks: Tip 12 body and head. Tip 2 beak and eyes.

Pigs: Tip 2A body and head; tip 10 legs, ears, and snout; tip 2 tail; tip 1 eyes and mouth.

Hippo: Tip 2A body and head; tip 12 legs and hat; tip 3 eyes, ears, mouth, pads of feet and pompon.

Bear: Tip 2A body and head; tip 12 legs and paws; tip 4 ears, tip 1 eyes, mouth, nose and pads of paws.

Turtles: Tip 2A body; tip 10 head and feet, tip 3 tail, tip 1 features.

Mice: Tip 12 body and ears, tip 4 nose and tail; tip 1 features.

Bunnies: Tip 12 body and heat, tip 8 legs, ears and paws; tip 1 features and tail.

Penguin uses tip 12 for body, head and wings. Tip 3 adds beak and feet. Pipe eyes with tip 1.

ribbon tips

pipe ribbons of icing in distinctive designs

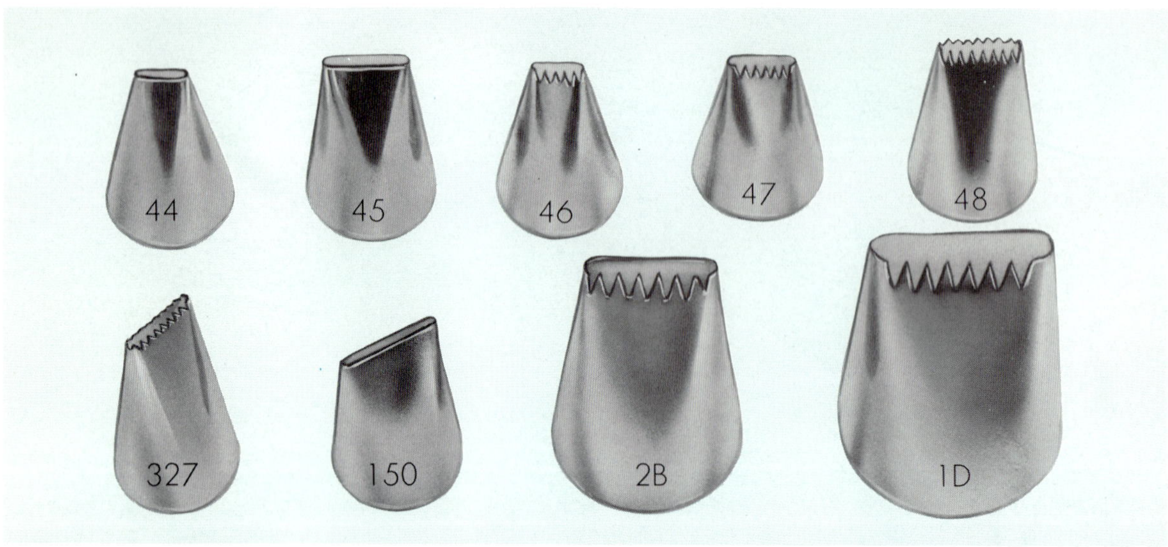

Ribbon tips come in 2 groups—straight and curved. Straight ribbon tips pipe tailored trims from tiny to large, which may be grooved or smooth. Straight ribbon tips may be used for borders and trims and most often are used for "basket weaving." Surprise the children with this delightful basket cake on Easter.

Using Candy Melts™ mold complete eggs (two halves put together), 7 or 8 half eggs, and bunny. (See the Complete Wilton Book of Candy, page 24, for directions.)

Bake, fill and ice a two-layer oval cake. Using tip 44, pipe a smooth vertical line from top to botom on side. With tip 2B, pipe three horizontal ribbed bars, about 2" wide and a tip width apart, across the vertical line. Pipe another tip 44 vertical line and repeat procedure to cover sides with basketweave. Add tip 48 shell-motion handles and border, and tip 233 "grass". Place eggs and bunny on top. Serves 12.

*brand confectionery coating

straight ribbon tips

do tailored trims

straight ribbon tips pipe trim and tailored borders and motifs. You'll achieve a completely different effect depending on whether you're holding the grooved side up or down.

Tip 44 and a shell motion do a "pleated border" for a cake top. Try it also for lettering or to build a fence around cake side.

Use tip 48 and a "C" motion for double-curve border. Yellow swag is tip 44.

See the difference in the two borders below. (Both need measuring and marking). The first is a smooth, simple tip 2B curve. The second places grooved side of tip 2B up and is done with a back-and-forth movement for a fluted effect.

Use grooved side of ribbon tip 1D for the simplest of top-edge borders. Tip 1D "C" motion and a dainty drop flower is all the trim a cake side needs.

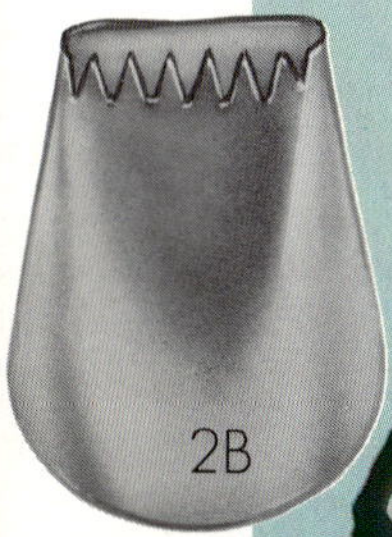

2B

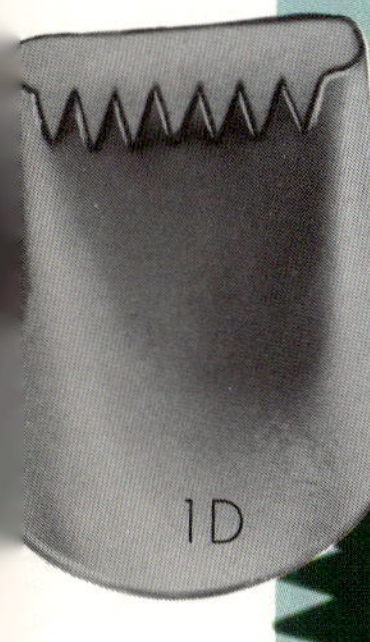

1D

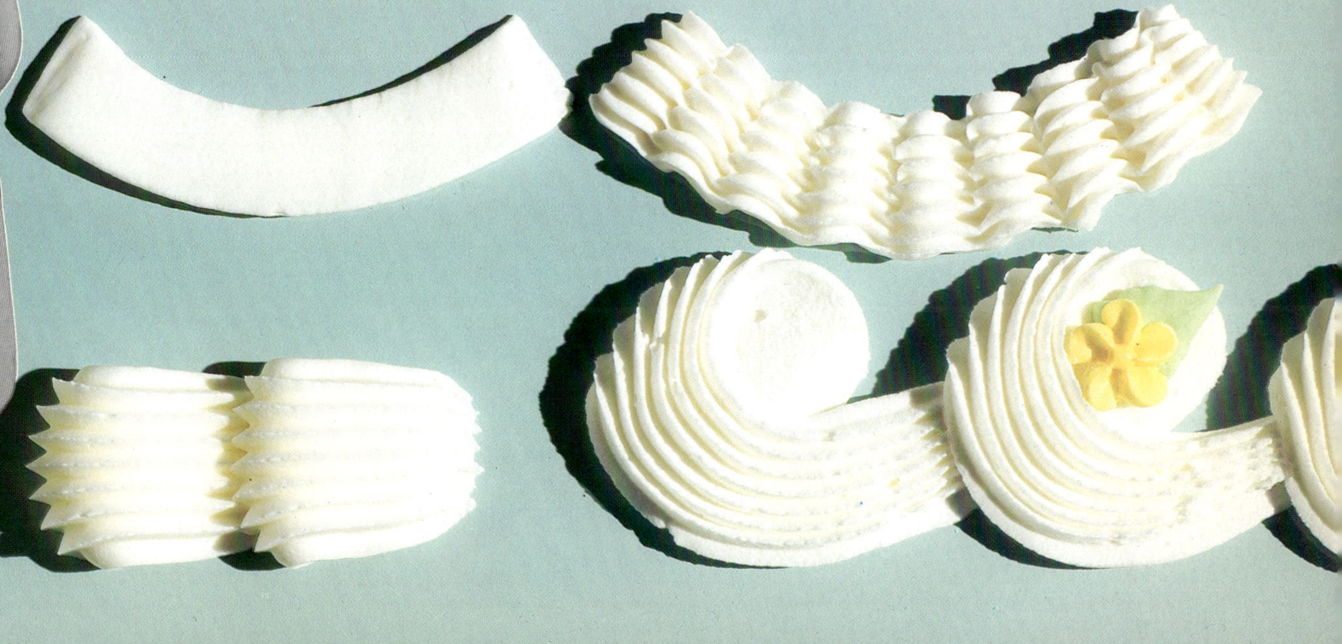

curved ribbon tips

pipe graceful curved designs—flowers, too

Sweeping curves, flounces, flourishes and flowers can be piped with the curved ribbon tips. These popular tips range in size from little to large and have crescent shaped openings.

The autumn mum is beautiful on layer or tiered cakes. Lovely for fall weddings in shades of orange, gold or even white, this small flower is piped with tip 79 and stiff royal icing to achieve a sharp petal effect. Hold bag at 90° angle to flower nail and pipe tip 6 mound of icing in center. Fit bag with tip 79; holding bag with half moon pointing up and at outer base of icing mound, squeeze row of cupped base petals using pull-out star method. Add second row of shorter petals in between those on first row. Repeat, making each row of petals shorter than the previous ones. End with a few stand-up petals on top and tip 1 center dot.

Tip 79

Tip 80

Water lily is piped in royal icing with tip 79 on a number 7 flower nail. Pipe a circle of six evenly-spaced petals lying flat on nail. Hold bag at 45° angle and pipe a row of five upstanding petals on previous row. Pinch tips of all petals to points with fingers dipped in cornstarch. Hold bag at 90° angle and pipe four cupped petals in center. Add a cluster of tip 1 stamens. Want smaller flowers? Use tip 80.

Curved ribbon tip borders are beautifully at home on bold handsome masculine cakes or flowery delightful feminine cakes. They produce an inwardly curving line, a ruffle or a swag that creates an exciting effect.

Double swag border is quick and easy. Add a tip 4 outline accent, tip 66 leaf, and made-ahead drop flower.

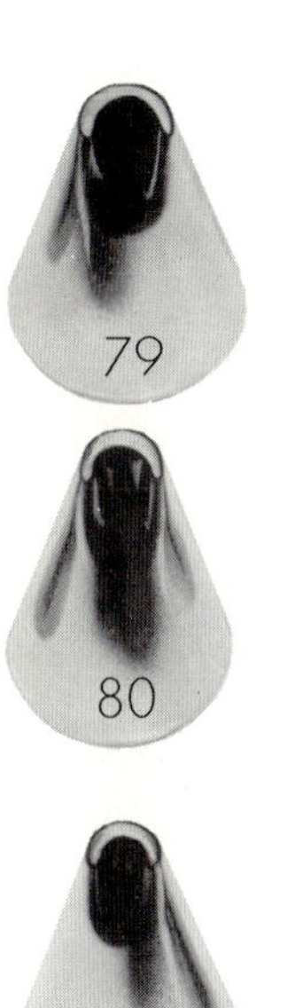

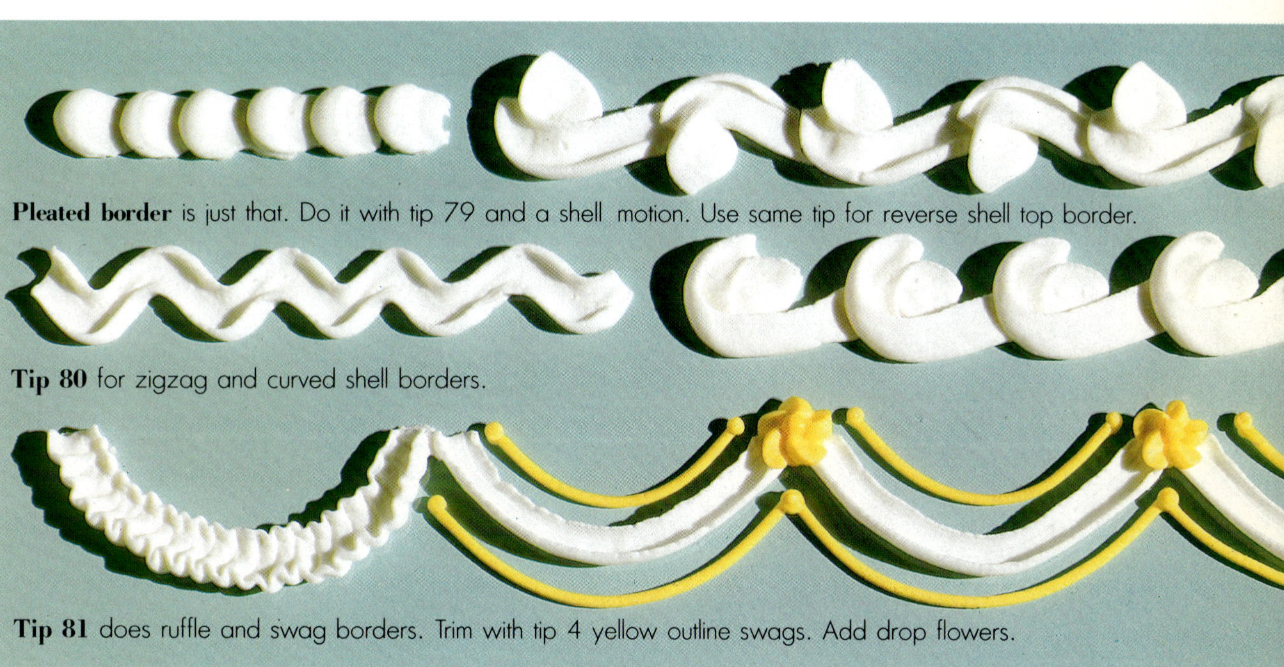

Pleated border is just that. Do it with tip 79 and a shell motion. Use same tip for reverse shell top border.

Tip 80 for zigzag and curved shell borders.

Tip 81 does ruffle and swag borders. Trim with tip 4 yellow outline swags. Add drop flowers.

Lace border is a real winner. Pipe a row of 79 "U" shapes.
Add a tip 79 "U" to center of each "U" above it. Lavish effect, quickly done.

scallops in chocolate

make the perfect all-occasion cake.

Everyone will love this big, wonderful chocolate cake. It's so easy to do with the bold straight ribbon tips. Just bake two 10" square layers. Fill and ice. With toothpick, mark 2-inch scallops on cake top, and 2½-inch scallops on cake side for bottom border. With tip ID, cover cake side marks. Use tip 45 for top scallops on side and cake top scallops. Write message and make outline scallops, dots and bows with tip 1. Serves 24.

a sweetheart of a cake

for showers, birthdays, mother's day, more!

Bake this beautiful cake in the 9" Happiness Heart pan. Decorate it in ruffles and swags with the graceful curved ribbon tips and you'll have a picture to remember for any occasion.

Fill and ice two-layer cake. In advance, make about 20 each, tip 23 and tip 224 royal icing drop flowers. With toothpick, mark C-shapes on cake top and scallops mid-way on cake sides. Edge cake top and bottom with tip 79 shell-motion border. Cover cake top scallop marks with tip 79. Cover cake side marks with tip 401 ruffle and top it with tip 401 swag. Add tip 2 message. Attach flowers, and trim with tip 66 leaves. Serves 14.

star tips

have multi uses

Star tips are the hardest workers of all the decorating tips. They execute fancy borders, pipe simulated flowers, do elaborate designs for tops or sides of cake—all in just a few minutes.

It's a good idea to practice piping with star tips since they are used so much. On these pages, we show you just a few ideas for decorative borders. You'll think of many more.

Star tips fall into three groups—standard open star tips, standard closed star tips and a special group of tips with unusually cut ends. All may be used somewhat interchangeably. The open and closed star tips are identical except for size, so it is very easy to learn to pipe with them.

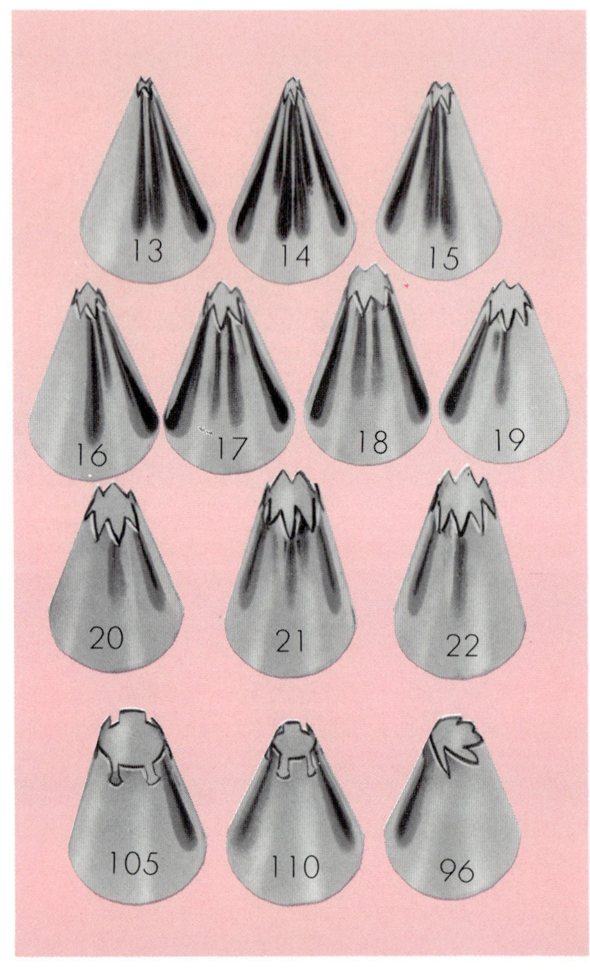

Fan border uses color contrast. With a toothpick, mark the fan lines, then the end points of the garland. Using tip 17, pipe the zigzag garlands, using very light pressure at ends, heavy pressure in center. Then pipe tip 13 fan outlines. Accent with tip 17 royal icing drop flowers (made ahead). Overpipe garland with tip 13.

Here we show you the standard tip 17 shell border. You'll use this border more than any other—it's fast, simple and versatile.

open star tips

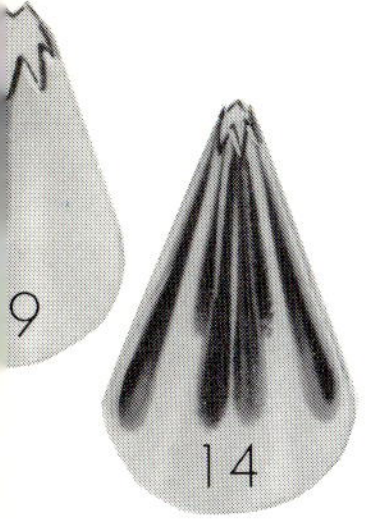

Use tip 19 to pipe two touching shells, overpipe them with tip 14.

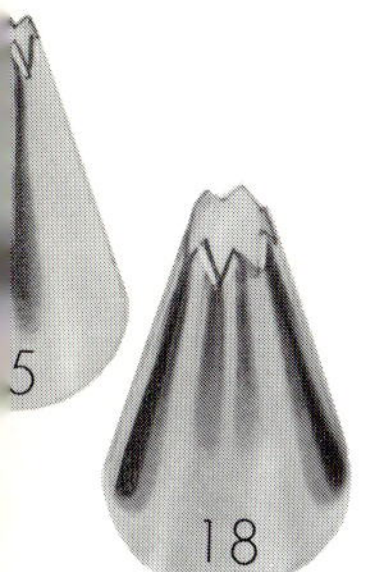

Pipe tip 15 reverse scrolls, add tip 18 drop flowers with tip 4 centers, tip 15 leaves.

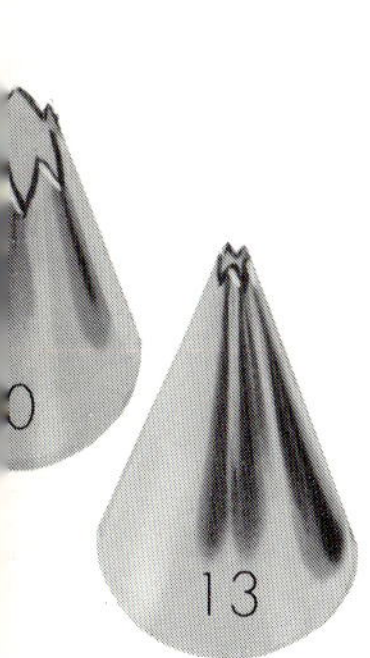

Do two touching tip 20 shells. Add third shell in center. Trim with tip 13 strings and stars.

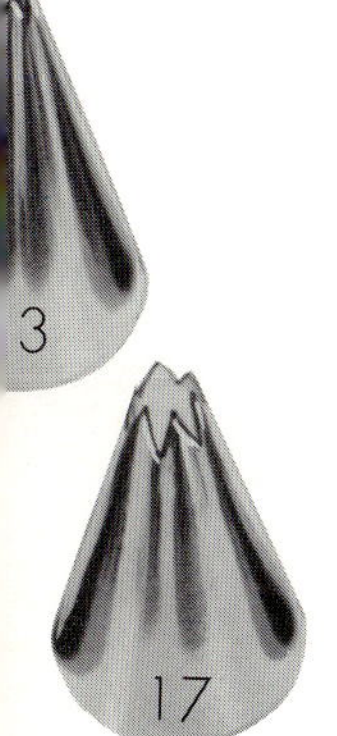

Measure carefully, then pipe continuous tip 13 scallops around the cake side.
Add tip 17 drop flowers and leaves.

cupid cake adds romance

Make ahead about 50 tip 33 and 10 tip 23 royal icing drop flowers with tip 2 centers. Fill and ice two layer, 10" round cake. Measure and mark cake into 12ths midway on side and on center top. (Mark sides for strings and base.) Outline center top and base marks with tip 2. Fill in center and base with tip 16 stars. Connect side marks with tip 13 drop strings. Trim with tip 16 rosettes. Edge cake top with tip 16 reverse shells. Attach tip 33 flowers to cake and tip 23 flowers to Frolicking Cherub with icing. Position cherub on cake top. Serves 24.

fine cut open star tips

produce refined designs

These tips are shaped like the standard open star tips, but their teeth are more numerous and finely cut, allowing them to create a sharp, refined effect. The curves produced with these tips are more accented and the stars have a button-like shape. Fine cut open star tips can be used for any of the techniques piped with standard open star tips as well as for special effects.

The designs shown here are nicely set off by color contrast. Use cookie cutters or pattern presses to guide piping.

Pipe two facing "C" curves with tip 199. Connect with two touching tip 364 shells.

Pipe a row of tip 363 "C"'s. Accent with tip 3 strings and dots.

closed star tips

pipe exciting designs and flowers

Here is a group of 14 tips, that are very easy to use. They do wonderful borders, top and side designs, and, surprise—a very pretty bachelor button! To make it, use royal icing and work on a square of waxed paper attached with icing to a flower nail. First, with tip 7, and bag at 90° angle to flower nail, squeeze out a circular mound of icing. Pull out a cluster of tip 25 stamens in center of mound. Add pull-out star petals around mound, starting at base. Repeat procedure as you move nail counterclockwise until mound is covered. Add random petals to finish gentleman's flower.

Some lovely border variations made with the closed star tips are shown on the next page. Use contrasting colors for marvelous effects. We've combined rosettes, garlands, swirls, zigzags and flowers (both swirled and plain) to create a multitude of icing designs.

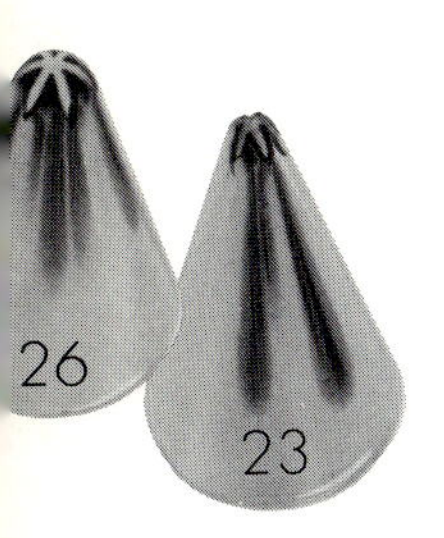

Whirligig. Pipe white rosettes with tip 26, overpipe pink rosettes with tip 23 accent.

Variations on a rosette. Pipe rosettes with tip 26, garlands with tip 23.

Rosette garland. Pipe tip 26 garland; add tip 23 rosette and trim with tip 66 leaves.

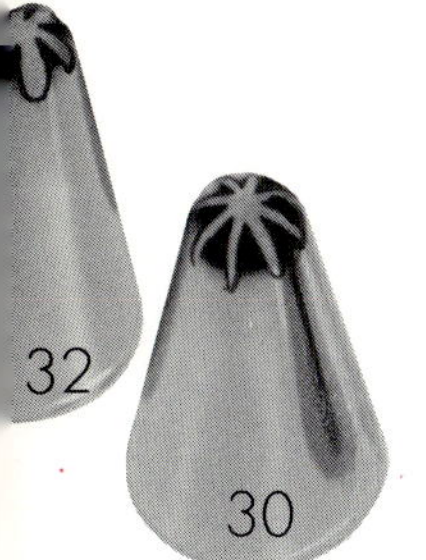

Flowers and swirls. Pipe tip 30 white swirls, then trim with tip 132 drop flowers with tip 2 centers and tip 66 leaves.

Zigzag and flower garland. First pipe tip 132 zigzag garland, then tip 132 alternating plain and swirled drop flowers with tip 2 centers. Trim with tip 1 dots.

A cake for the groom

The groom will appreciate a cake of his own, especially one adorned with symbolic "bachelor" buttons—like this one.

Make ahead about 38 royal icing bachelor buttons. To make, see p. 34.

Bake, fill and ice a two-layer 10" square cake. Midway on each side, mark 2 inches in from corners, for pillars. Using a round cookie cutter, mark scallop design on top. Write tip 4 message. Then pipe tip 25 scallops on cake top. Starting from bottom, pipe tip 22 pillars. Edge cake bottom and top with tip 25 shells. Connect pillars on sides with tip 23 strings. Top pillars with tip 23 rosettes. Attach flowers with dots of icing.

star tips and pattern presses

make big impressions oh so fast!

The design on these 10″ round cakes are imprinted with pattern presses and cookie cutters, then quickly outlined. By combining these handy timesavers, the possibilities are endless.

Heart to heart. Imprint with a pattern press. Outline with tip 16. Add tip 21 rosette. Edge top with tip 16 shell border, bottom with tip 18 shell border. Attach tip 35 drop flowers with tip 2 centers and tip 352 leaves.

Flowery curves. Defined with a pattern press, these lovely designs are outlined with tip 14. Add tip 14 shell top border and tip 18 shell bottom border. Attach tip 225 drop flowers and trim with tip 349 leaves.

Curves in the square. A combination of pattern presses outlined with tip 362, and tip 364 shell borders creates the frame for this lovely cake top. Add tip 35 drop flowers with tip 2 centers and tip 352 leaves.

Sweetheart. Just press a heart cutter on the cake top and outline with tip 14. Add tip 14 scallops and shell top border and tip 18 shell bottom border.

star-cut tips pipe sharply cut forms

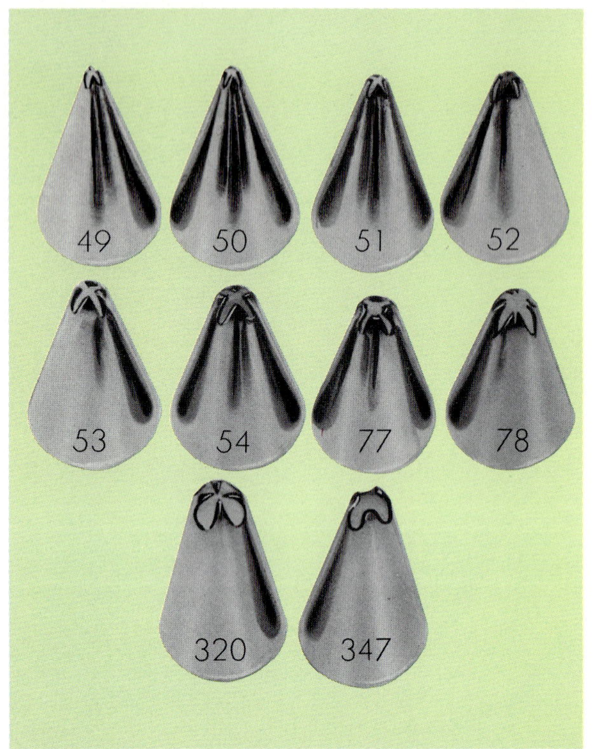

The rolled fondant cake shown below is trimmed with cross tips 52 and 54. To make: Ahead of time, make tip 52 royal icing drop flowers with tip 2 centers. Bake, fill and ice a 9" two-layer hexagon cake. Cover with satiny rolled fondant, then mark cake and top and side with a round cookie cutter, centering it on each side of the hexagon. Cover marks with tip 54 ruffly garlands. Connect circles with tip 52 single garlands. Edge cake base with tip 54 shell border. Trim single garlands with tip 67 leaves. Attach flowers to single garlands and inside circles with dots of icing.

Fleurs-de-lis and flowers. Pipe tip 77 fleur-de-lis, then add little curves of make-ahead tip 54 drop flowers with tip 2 piping gel centers.

Star-cut shell chain. Pipe a row of tip 347 shells. Add tip 3 golden shell centers.

Star-cut "C" border. The strong cuts of tip 320 give this border a lot of power. Add tip 3 string accent.

Fluffy ruffle motif. Measure and mark for this. Pipe lower garlands with tip 54, garlands above with tip 51. Attach tip 54 drop flowers with tip 2 piping gel centers.

star-cut tips can produce unusual effects

Here's a basket cake that's fun to decorate with the unusually cut star-cut tips. A basket of flowers tops a classical cake for a different look. Start by making ahead of time, about two dozen each tips 1B, 2D, 190 and 193 royal icing drop flowers with tip 2 pull-out stamens. Also make about one dozen tip 131 drop flowers with tip 2 dot centers. Bake a one-layer 6″ cake. Bake, fill and ice a two-layer 10″ cake. Place 6″ cake on cake board and pipe tip 62 shells in rows around sides for "basket" effect. Place cake atop 10″ cake. Measure and mark 10″ cake into 10ths. Edge 10″ cake with tip 62 shell borders. Pipe tip 88 ruffle garlands between marks, then tip 88 swags above ruffles. Mound pink icing on top of small cake to build up center. Place flowers on mound. Attach tip 131 flowers to sides. Trim with tip 352 leaves. Serves 28.

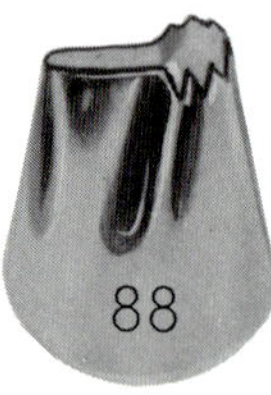

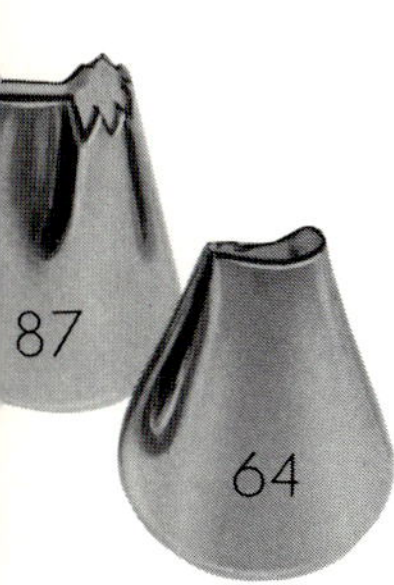

Double rosebud. A tip 64 shell makes a pretty rosebud with just one squeeze. Trim tip 87 ruffle garlands with rosy pairs.

Rickrack border looks neat and trim. Do rickrack with tip 88, bead hearts with tip 3.

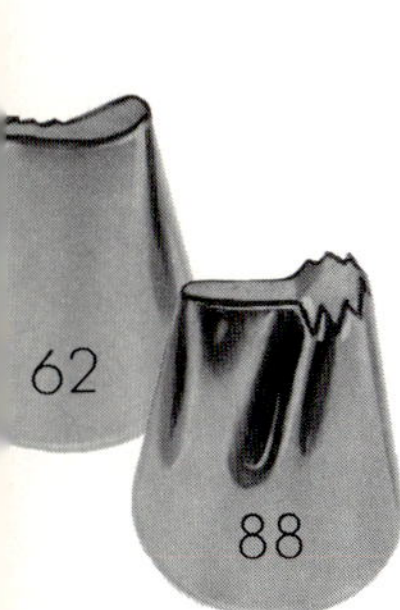

Double swag is bold and flowing. Pipe larger swag with tip 88, smaller with tip 62. Trim with tip 224 drop flowers with tip 2 centers.

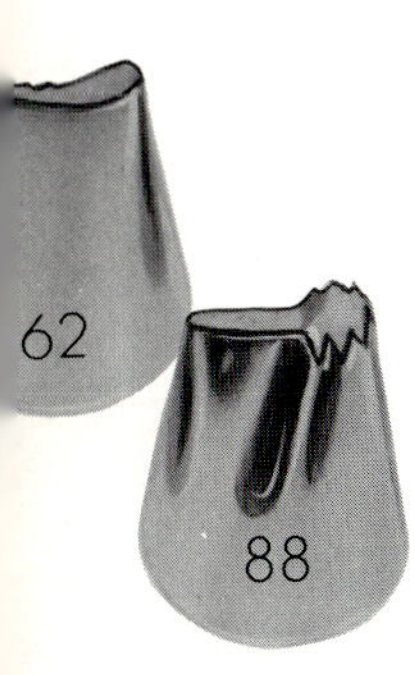

Baby rosebud border adds grace and daintiness. Pipe an e-motion swag with tip 88. Using tip 2, outline stems. Add tip 62 "shell" rosebuds. Trim with tip 2 calyx, sepals and tip 352 leaves.

star-cut tips

flower an Easter cake.

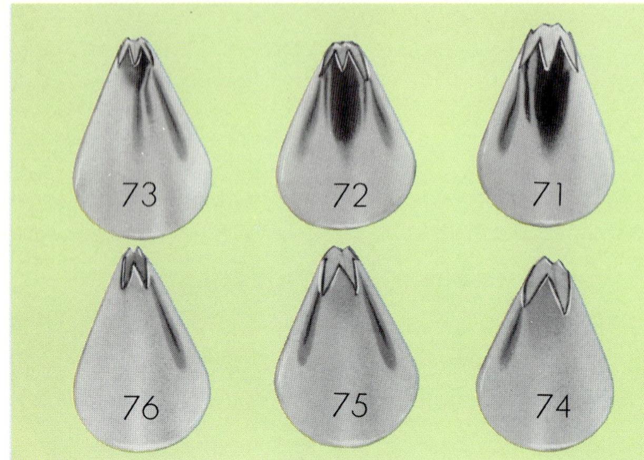

Let the petal shape guide you when marking scrolls on top and sides of the two-layer 12" cake on the opposite page. Make ahead about 35 tip 74 royal icing lilies and 8 tip 75 lilies (see below right). Ice cake. Edge base with tip 73 shell border. Pipe tip 71 C-scrolls on top and sides. Edge top with tip 74 two-toned double ruffles (stripe bag with ½ green and ½ white icing). Write tip 1 message. Attach lilies on mounds of icing. Add tip 66 leaves. Serves 28.

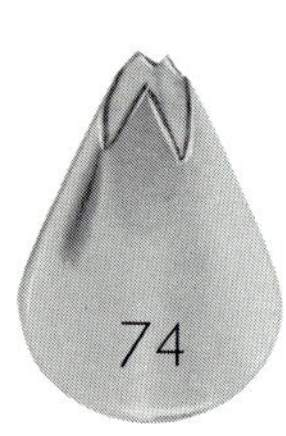

Measure and mark your cake side: then try a curved ruffled border with tip 74, adding tip 66 leaves.

Use tip 74 for this shell-motion border. Doesn't it look different? Reverse sides to make two different designs.

Reverse "C" curves for a strong side-of-cake border. Pipe them with tip 72.

Easter lily. Pipe these beautiful blooms in a 1⅝" two-piece lily nail lined with foil. With tip 74 (75), touch center well of nail, squeeze and pull out three long petals, evenly spaced with pointed tips. Pipe three more petals, one between each of the first three. Press a tip 14 star in the center and add 5 artificial yellow stamens. Lift out flower and foil to dry.

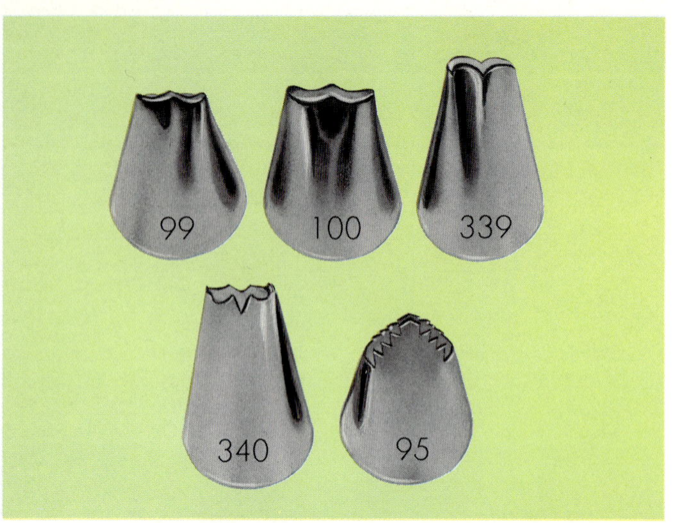

star-cut tips

with center ridges

Here are some unusual tips that are completely different from any other. Each will pipe a design uniquely characteristic of its form. The borders shown here are just small samples of the many wonderful designs these tips can pipe.

Loop the loop. Trim a tip 340 garland border with tip 3 double loops.

Change hand positions and tip 340 creates a curved shell border.

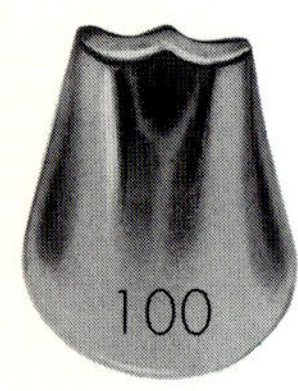

Ruffle over swag goes together quickly on a cake side. Measure and mark midway on cake side. Tip 100 does the piping.

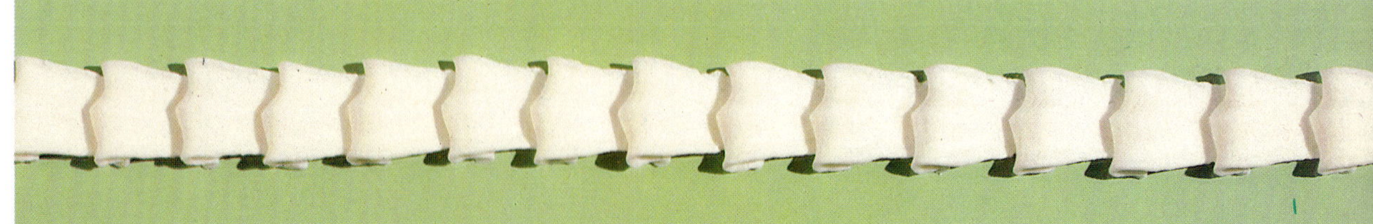

Neat pleats are easy to pipe with shell-motion and tip 100.

special use tips

This group of tips really does not fit in with any other groups—each has its own special use. Experiment with them—they're great to use.

Irish hearts are easy to pipe with tip 353. Just one squeeze pipes a perfect heart. Set three together, add a tip 2 stem—a shamrock. Use the same tip for a shell-motion pleated border.

Use tip 301 for a message. Perfect for "flat" lettering.

Tip 2010 does the work of several. Pipes three stars at one time.

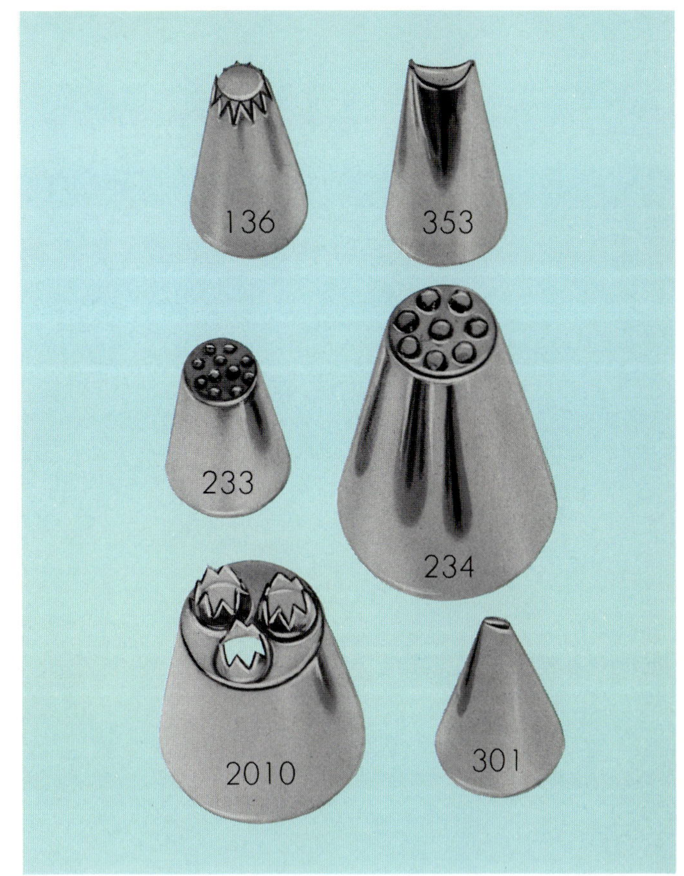

giant tips pipe speedy trims; give dramatic effects to cake, pastries

The giant tips pipe forms identical to those of smaller tips, only larger. With these big tips you can turn out a tray of fancy pastries or a lovely celebration cake—and do it in a hurry. Turn to these tips when you have a really rush job.

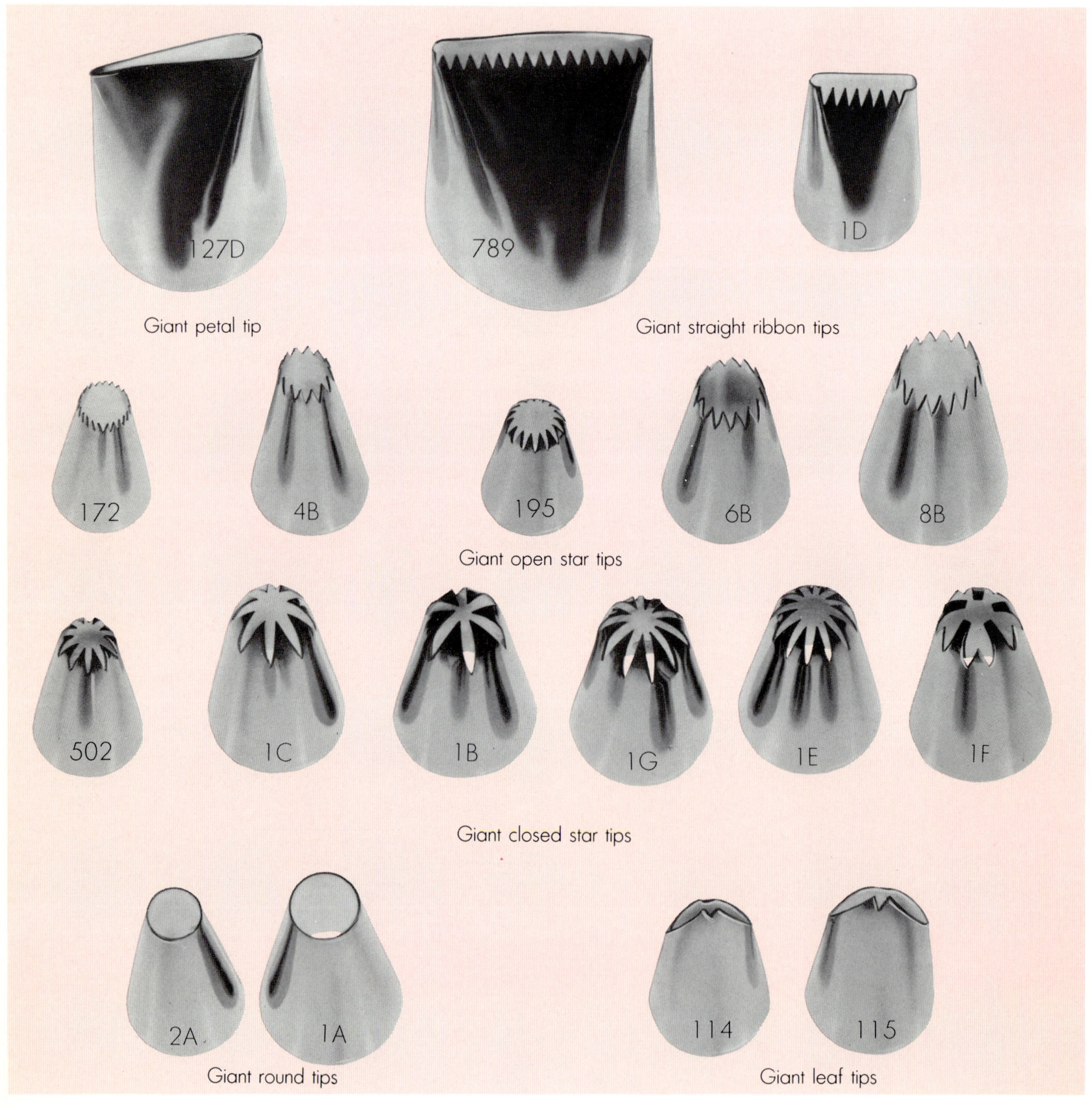

Giant petal tip

Giant straight ribbon tips

Giant open star tips

Giant closed star tips

Giant round tips

Giant leaf tips

Ring of Flowers Cake. Bake, fill and ice a two-layer, 8" cake. Divide into 16ths. Pipe 16 tip 195 swirls at bottom for border. Edge cake top with 16 tip 114 leaves. Add tip 1F drop flowers with tip 1 pull-out dot centers. Pipe 6 tip 1F flowers with tip 114 leaves in center. Serves 12.

Fancy cookies. (You can tint the dough for a prettier effect.) At the lower part of tray are simple shells piped with tip 195. Above them, tip 6B swirls, done just like a swirled flower. Then a flower, piped with tip 1F held straight up. At the very top are bar cookies done with grooved ribbon tip 1D. After baking, dip the ends into melted Candy Melts™, then in chopped nuts. Garnish with nuts, cherries, citron pieces.

* confectionery coating

Now that we've shown you the wonderful capabilities of the most popular decorating tips, you can enjoy discovering the beautiful possibilities.

Ribbon and Petal Tips combine to create a wedding cake that's simply divine!

1. With white royal icing, make 10 roses on no. 7 flower nail and 70 sweet peas with tip 104. Let dry.

2. Bake, fill and ice 2-layer round cakes—6" x 3", 8" x 4" and 12" x 4". Position on cake circles, 7" separator plate and foil-covered base. Dowel rod and stack 8" and 12" tiers. Divide top tier into 4ths, base tier into 8ths.

3. Pipe vertical ribbed bars at marks and a horizontal bar around center of 8" tier with tip 1D. Edge base with tip 104 ruffles. Outline separator plate with tip 16 scallops. Pipe tip 16 shell borders on tops, tip 32 shells at bases. Attach flowers to tops, sides and separator plate with dots of icing. Pipe tip 3 outline vines on separator plate. Trim flowers with tip 352 leaves. Assemble top tier on 3" Grecian Pillars. Accent with Petite Elegance. These pretty tiers will serve 81 guests.